Playing the Game of Futures & Options

How about you
win for a change ?

Your rulebook to
Win

Bill Lucre

First Published in **September 2024**

ISBN: 978-93-6356-032-1

PUBLISHING MONGERS

+91 9311101365

Distributed by: Watergies

Preface

A market where while trading futures and options, loss is not an option. A market where you outsmart the market by depending on some factors that help you win. A rule book that tells it all, protects you all the way and makes you money all the time, time being critical.

Foreword

The author gives you a nice insight into the world of Futures and Options where he also tells you about how to navigate different situations with different methods and strategies. Trading is not a perfect world, but with knowledge and help as such mentioned in the book, it can become a lot easier and a lot safer.

Acknowledgments

A heartfelt thanks to the publishing team for everything you have done for me and investors all across the globe.

About the author

Just an investor who learnt it all with experience.

Dedication

This one is for every investor who trades in futures and options and for whom loss in not an acceptable option.

Introduction

When trading futures and options, if you stick to a certain set of rules, you will probably never lose money. You won't become a billionaire in a day, but how about you know when to enter a trade and when to avoid it. How about you know how to eliminate the risk altogether. If not eliminate it, minimise it. Also know when you can earn exponentially and when a small gain is better than the risk. This is your rulebook for trading futures and options, and how about you win for a change while Playing the Game of Futures and Options.

Prologue

Remember to make a mistake, but this mistake should not be so big a blunder, that you can never afford to make another mistake.

So, you want to dabble in the world of futures and options, how about you stop losing money and start winning for a change.

It requires discipline. Do you have it ?

No, it is not difficult, it is frankly much easier, but you have to play tactfully. You have to be strict about when you want to take a low risk high reward trade, and when you want to take a low risk low reward trade.

You might often be rewarded in a high risk trade, but there is an equal chance to lose. If the rush of the game is what you seek, this guide is probably not for you. If your goal is to never lose, and gain exponentially, you are in the right place.

Remember it is your money, no one in the market cares about it other than you. If you make a foolish move, it is just you who loses and the market won't care. If you win, it won't care even then.

Follow these simple rules on the basis of your preferences, and you will always have the upper hand.

Always sell, always sell hedged and never buy, unless ..

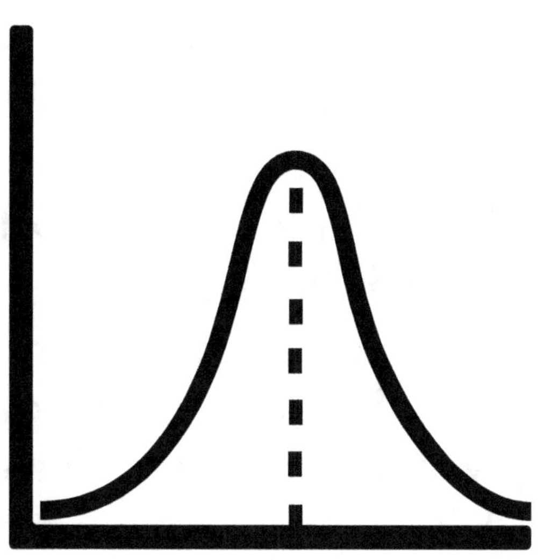

Is the market Bearish or Bullish ?

Be the bull with a bearish sentiment, and a bear with a bullish sentiment

Are you a bear or a bull ? Nobody cares. If you are a bull, that does not mean the market is or will be bullish. Same, even if you are a bear. Open up the charts for a year, and take a look how much the market is growing every month. If you see a substantial growth over the year, or an average growth over a month, you have your answer. Since the global markets are in a bullish trajectory, let us assume you came to a bullish conclusion. Now, that does not mean you become a permabull. There will be corrections, there will be news impacts, there will be profit bookings, there will be major stock falls. All of that can keep happening, and it should not impact you a single bit. Yes, you should not be concerned about any of it, but you should be expecting it, waiting for it to happen, so that you can enter. In a bullish market, if you want a low risk high reward trade, you should be wishing for it every night before you go to sleep. You do not have to just take a bullish bear trade or a bearish bull trade, but you are never going to miss it. Now, it opens up every opportunity to you. You need to evaluate the fall. The more, the merrier. Wherever the market was, that is your expected goal, it might take a few weeks, it might take a few days or it might be there tomorrow, but in a bullish market, the market is getting there and no one can stop it. Now, what is it you want ? You want an equal loss and an equal gain win ? You win that amount on the day of the expiry with just a single point in your favour, or do you want to ride every single point for the win, this is all upto you and your appetite. You can take a look at various strategies and figure out what your goal is, but as long as you have time i.e. you enter a little far dated, preferably in an expiry a month away, you are golden. But, remember to never go in naked. Always remain hedged, always protect yourself against an uncertainty. Remember to make a mistake, but this mistake should not be so big a blunder, that you can never afford to make another mistake. There can be a terrorist attack, a president can die, a country can go to war, anything, everything that is out of your control. You cannot take a trade based on it, but you can always buy insurance against it by hedging your trade. Never buy, never sell, always strategise. A simple call buy and a put sell combination opens you up to exponential gains if you are right, but finishes your bank account if you are wrong. Whereas, if you add in an extra put buy to the combination, your gains still remain exponential, but it protects you against uncertainties. Your goal is to earn, but never with unlimited losses or giving into theta decay. You have to win at your own terms, and yes you can.

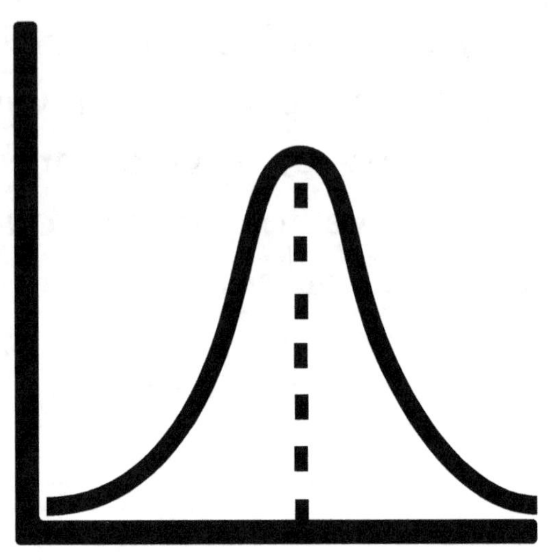

Are you in for the
Long Game ?

If you want an exit from your
trade today, get out right now.
You probably won't get it here

You are not here to gamble, you are going to go for a far dated contract expiry, and not risk anything for today. You cannot control what happens in the market today. About the entries and exits in your trades, you are going to enter in today, but your target exit is at least a month away. You do not have to exit a month away, but you need to have that in your favour. You need to let intrinsic value and time value work in your favour. Now, the choices available for you will be simple. You enter in the morning, you take a trade. It could be anything, a bearish trade, a bullish trade, a neutral trade, none of it matters. By the closing, you have to evaluate what you have gained. If the market did not move or stay in your direction, it does not matter, even if intrinsic is not supporting you, time is going to come out soon to support you. And intrinsic is fickle, but if you have time, it will come back, it always does. Now, in an alternate case, if you were able to get your hand around intrinsic today itself, you did not require the help of time value, you can exit, book your profits and take another trade tomorrow. The longer you have stayed in the trade, the more potential you have to earn. The choice is entirely yours, not like while buying an option where if you stay in a trade, you lose money every second. Here, you earn money every second. The more you stay in, the merrier is your stay. While selling hedged options, the choice of exiting your trade is upto you, you can exit it in a minute, in an hour, in a day or in a month. It all depends on how much you want to risk and how much do you want to earn, and you are going to be rarely ever wrong because the market always moves, and you will be in your sweet range at one time or the other.

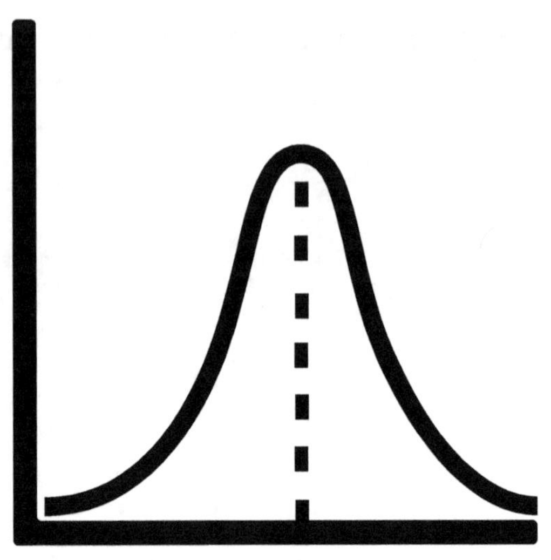

How much you want to risk ?

Rather how much can you afford to risk ?

You need to know what it is you can afford to lose. With all the strategies, all the precautions, all the hedges, there is still a risk. That risk is calculated to the best of our abilities, but markets work on infinite factors, every little thing across the world impacts the market, and you can never quantify it all, especially if it is an unexpected extraordinary event that has almost never happened before. So, you have to ask yourself, what if something like that happens, it probably won't, but what if it does. All you can do is protect yourself against it, and build that wall. The only way to build it is to hedge yourself. Now, hedging comes in all forms and sizes. The choice is completely yours. For a trade where you are selling an At The Money call option, the hedge can be approximately equal to your potential profit. While if you are building a synthetic future, your hedge can take its toll. A lot depends on how confident you are about your trade. If you are sure, you are at the bottom and you add the time advantage to the mix, to let it work for you along with intrinsic, the odds are favourable, but on the other side of the coin, you have to look at the what if. What if another event happens somewhere far away that really breaks the market's sentiment. You need to be prepared for it. Never risk more than you can afford to lose. You need to have the ability to risk again, if things go wildly wrong. And, they will. They always do at least once in every trader's life. It usually happens because of an extraordinary circumstance, rather than a trader's mistake, but it happens. Remember the covid crisis ? Or the financial crisis ? No one could have known that, and imagine the life of a trader who had sold a put, maybe even ten percent away. It does not matter who was responsible, you need to be hedged and hedged to the extent where you can absorb the blunder, not that you are expecting that to happen in any way, you are not here to gamble, this is the last resort, but if it does, you should be able to absorb it, and then make money on the rise. With the hedge, you can lose only a specific amount, but while gaining on a roll, there is nothing stopping you. There needs to be money left to afford the ride back up.

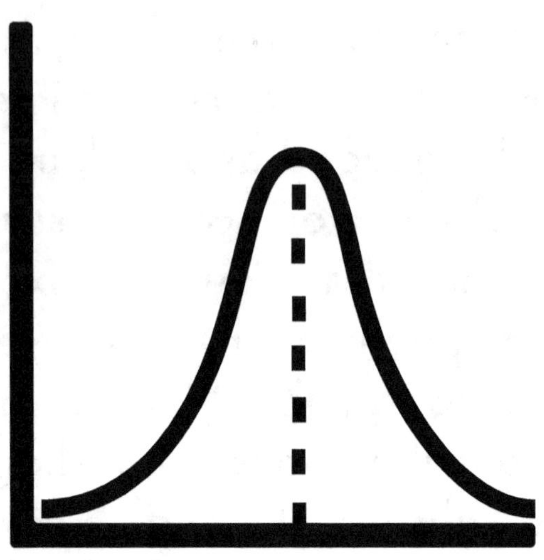

What do you want ?

An assured amount or do you
want to earn with every point in
your favour ?

Before you are making a trade, you need to ask yourself, where do you see the market by the time of your contract's expiry, and how confident are you about it ? You need to ask yourself whether you want some guaranteed points even if the market moves ten percent in your direction, or do you want to go on the ride collecting every point you can. Now, both the directions are right, you can't go wrong either way, but you need to know what you want with no regrets. If you are going for a specific guaranteed amount, you win the game with just one point in your favour. But, that is only temporary. Your assured gain is building up, but you can only grab all of it if you wait till the end or the intrinsic helps you out. If the market moves substantially in your direction, you get your assured reward, otherwise even in the win zone, you are going to have to wait to grab it all. And, if you are just at the border, there is an additional worry of what if I am wrong, and you can easily become wrong on day zero, even if it is temporary. Now, if you are riding the ride for every point, the only advantage you have here is that you get rewarded for every point in your direction. It works wonders after a correction. Here, time becomes irrelevant. There is no decay, and you get rewarded for every point. There are lots of strategies that help you achieve that, but let's try the synthetic future again. If you go in naked, you gain with every point and you lose with every point. If you hedge, you still gain with every point in your direction. The risk is higher inspite of the hedge in comparison to an assured amount, but the reward is much better, even at lower margins and hedged losses. The choice again is yours as to how confident are you in your trade, what is the move you predict, how much is it, how much do you want to risk, how much you want to gain. We will get into strategies later, but the concept remains all the same.

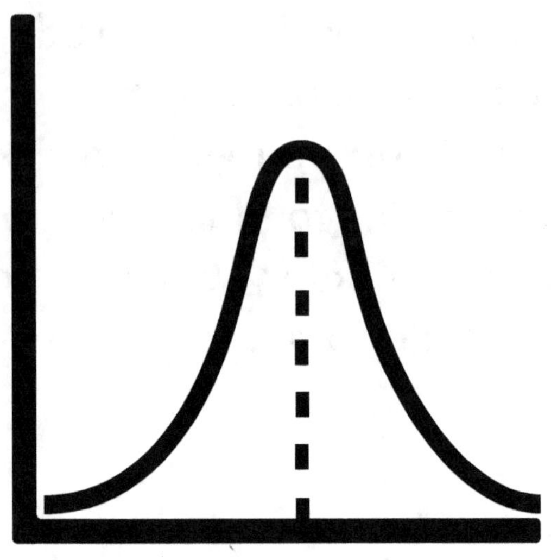

Never ever buy

Unless ..

You have an urge to buy. Everyone does. It is easy money. You buy something and in a minute, you can easily earn ten percent, with luck favouring you, an hundred percent with things really moving, and in a rare occasion, a thousand percent. But, it is similarly easy to lose it all, and that too, not because you were wrong, but just because you were early. For buying, you need to have the perfect entry and the perfect exit, because time is not your friend here. But there is one circumstance where buying can work out for you. You should only buy after a major correction, and that too only when the premium on your At the Money option is lesser than your expectation. Here, you can control time. Let's say the premium for the At the Money call option is much lesser than where the market was. You buy the call for a month or two away and wait. If the market decides to go back to where it was today, you earn wonders. If it decides to head in that direction today, again wonders. If the market decides to go in that direction in the coming days, you get a good profit. But, even if it takes the next two months to get there, your bet has been on intrinsic, you still earn. Now, in this case, the earlier the market gets there, the more premium you earn, but even if takes some frustrating time to get there, you still earn. You are still protected. You still make a profit. You also have the additional advantage of buying the same call option at a lower price, averaging down your buy, increasing your profit. But, be aware to not get carried away. Once you start averaging, your buy price keeps coming down, but time keeps breaking you down, and if the market does not move in your direction for a while, you would be so overbought, that the next decay is going to break your psychology, and rather than looking for a profit, you would be looking for an exit, and that is where you make a loss. Average out only when it makes a difference, and limit that down too. Buy only to the point you can afford to lose it all. Once you exceed that, the market controls the game, and more likely than not, you won't wait for the intrinsic, and you will exit at the first sign of a limited loss you can afford. And, ask any trader, as soon as you exit, the market will take your direction and all you would be left is with regret. Averaging out is good, but only to the point you can happily hold it and afford to lose it.

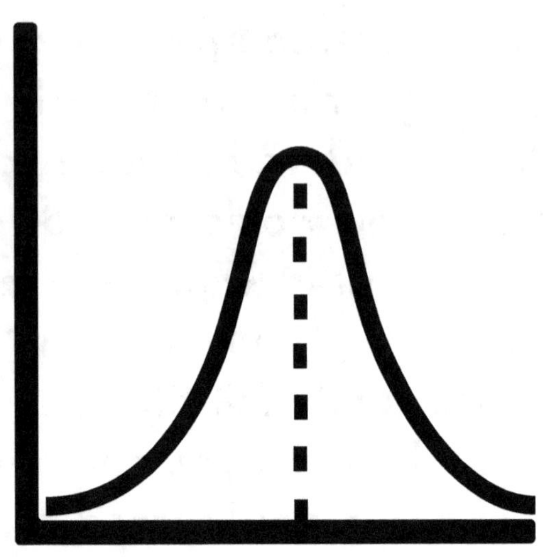

Having Bad Luck or Good Luck ?

It won't matter

Until now, have you been having bad luck with futures and options ? Or maybe some good luck, that too sometimes, because it never lasts. Well, now it should not matter, because none of it will be based on luck anymore. You are going to be earning irrespective of your luck. Everyone has faced a situation where they have run out of time in their trade and the contract expires. You are going to be immune from that, because you are going to sell options a month or two months apart, and target your exit, maybe tomorrow, maybe next week, or maybe by the end of the month. Whenever you exit, you will be profitable. The more you wait, the more you earn. It might happen sometimes that you are rangebound or bullish, and the market suddenly reverses direction. Firstly, it is recommended to enter in an already corrected market. Secondly, even if you are dabbling with rangebound trades, you have no hurry to be correct. Even if the market reverses direction, and you are adamant on the bullishness, you just need to wait and watch. The more time it spends there, you are stuck in that trade and you would not exit. Here, intrinsic is not yet working for you, but time is doing its part. After a week, or two weeks, when the market comes back in your profitable range, you would have earned much more than you would have had you exited the trade earlier. Even if you are impatient to stay in a trade on your own, the market will keep you in it and reward you along with it. The market will work to make you earn. There would be no sense in taking a trade where you have a target that cannot be achieved anytime even in the next two months.

You have to be realistic, and you will be rewarded. It is highly enjoyable to sell a deep Out of the Money put option, of course hedged, and it pays accordingly, but it has to be achievable, it has to be realistic. On a side note, if you plan your trade well, and sell a deep OTM option, you might start earning much before that, you need to evaluate that in the strategies, and figure out what works best for you.

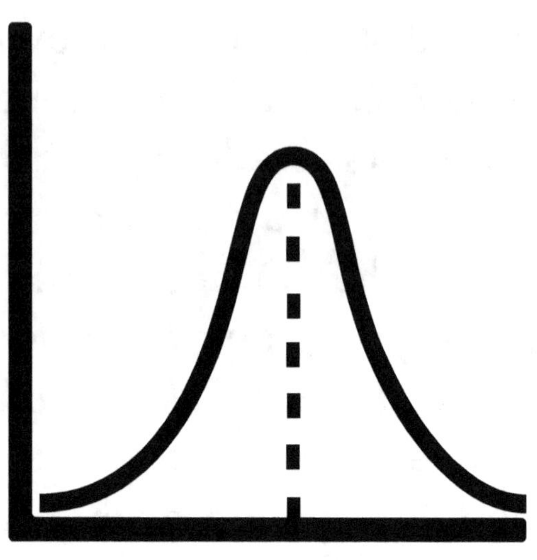

Patience or Exit

What do you think ?

Patience; futures and options is all about patience. Once you are in a trade, how patient do you want to be, that is upto you. Before you go in a trade, you do predict the markets heading, and even if you are not wrong, that is the market does not move, you start earning money. Now, if you are wrong, you have no choice but to stay in the trade, let it ride. But, if you are right, and let's say your potential earning target is high, but you have achieved a fraction of it, what do you do ? Do you ride it until the end ? You will have to evaluate your trade to reach a conclusion. If the trade has worked wonders for you, and the market has headed a lot in your direction, you have the margin for a minor correction. Intrinsic is already in your favour, and time is still playing in your team. You can sit back, and enjoy the ride. You just have to define a strict exit, that is where you exit if the market reverses direction, no matter how sure you are of the market heading again in your direction. But, what if the trade is on the border of your profit and loss, and right now, in the profit side, what do you do ? Here, the intrinsic has done its part, brought you ahead of the finish line, but time is still playing. The more you stay, the more you earn. But, if the market reverses its direction, intrinsic goes back into the stands, and time becomes useless. So, do you ride it or do you exit ? In this case, it is better to exit. Yes, you might earn more, a lot more if you stay, but you can lose what you have already earned, and a lot more. You should book your profits, and take another trade whenever you are comfortable. Nobody says that you always need to be in a trade. Trade only when you are comfortable, sure or highly positive about the heading of the market. You might have many factors like hedge, time, risk in your favour, but you need to be eventually right. All these factors become redundant if you are completely wrong. You can have the time to be correct, but you need to reach that correct for you to win.

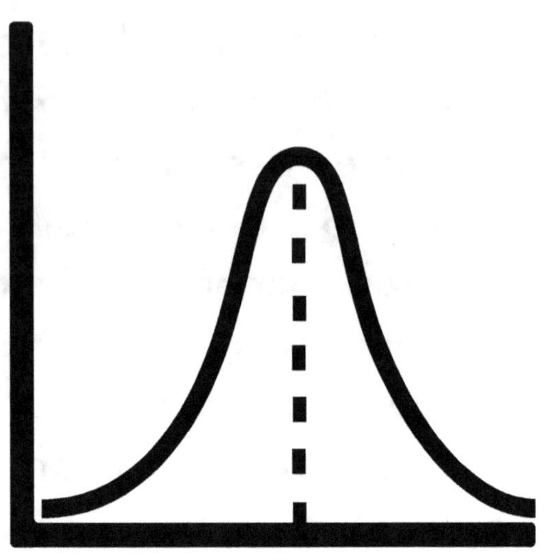

Never back out

Never ever

If you are getting in trade, you are not getting there to be wrong. You have the margin of time, and even if you are wrong, very wrong, you can be right again in a single day. If you have entered a trade with a bullish view on the current spot price, it is a relatively safe trade, because all you need is one point in your favour at the expiry. But, what if the market completely reverses direction, loses a few percent, and the future looks bleak. You lose your morale and look towards a loss on the trade. You wish you had entered at the current spot price, and that would have been a definite win. Now, what you need to do is, at this lower spot price, repeat that bullish trade, but with the current levels. In most cases, as soon as the market crosses this spot price, your loss becomes zero. Now, you are in that trade with nothing to gain, so you might think you should exit as soon as you see a shred of green, or rather a zero. But, you need to stay in that trade if you had confidence on the trade when you initially got into it. Your new trade is giving you all it can, but no matter how farfetched your former trade seems, it will eventually get there, all you need is time and you should have ample of it. In an alternate case, if you are breakeven and are still sure of the bullish trajectory, at the current levels. Exit the trades at zero and go in fresh. You saved your losses, booked your profits and you are still fighting for finally gaining after tallying up your trades. All that matters is that how confident were you initially when you got into your first trade. You need to be sure of your trades or there is nothing and no one that can protect you from your losses. Market may take either direction once you enter in, but if you were right, market will come back to reward you every single time. It is only you who can lose your money, no one else. That goes for the gain too. Remember that, and you will have no problem in the market.

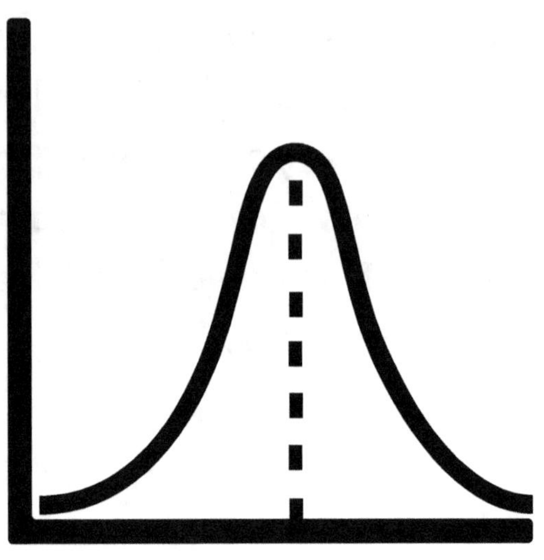

Never fight the market

No matter how right you think you are

You can never fight the market, no matter how right you are. You have to have patience, you can double down at times while keeping composure, but you can never fight the market. If you have taken a bullish trade at the current spot price, and you are sure of the direction, but due to profit book or an event, the market changes direction and turns bearish, you need to just wait and watch. You cannot keep repeating the same trade just because you are getting it cheaper. Averaging out in futures and options is a really bad idea, because unlike stocks, you do not have unlimited time. Granted, you are taking your trades with ample time in your corner, but can you be sure that there is not even one percent chance that the market does not take your direction in the time you have till expiry. You definitely cannot. Yes, you can be positive about it, but you cannot guarantee it. If the market falls, you cannot keep taking a new bullish trade at every interval it breaches because you do not know how far down it is searching. If the market changes direction in your favour again, you will earn at every interval, but you have to account for the what if. What if it does not. The best case strategy if you want to still be bullish and enter in multiples is, wait for the fall to settle. It usually settles within a day to a week. You will know when you see it. Here, the market falls a little, tries to recover some points, falls more, recovers again and finds a support. Here, the market is going to spend some time, and that is where you enter. You remember how many times you wanted to enter until now, and if you want to, enter in those multiples at the current spot price, or in all those trades where you wanted to enter before. You would have been in a notional loss in all those trades, had you entered before. But, now there is almost negligible scope of a loss, and all you are going to encounter is profit. More profit than you could have possibly gotten before, and no wait time. Since the market betrayed you a little, intrinsic was biting you up and time was redundant. It had been doing its job, but against you until now. If you enter in all those trades now, you will get the benefit of what time has been doing plus the intrinsic, and that too exponentially. So, never fight the market even if you are in a trade. Wait for the opportunity to get back in with some strength. You might miss a few trades this way, and you might regret the caution, but the goal here is not to risk it, but create a secure trade that might give you less, might give you more, but it should not take away anything from you.

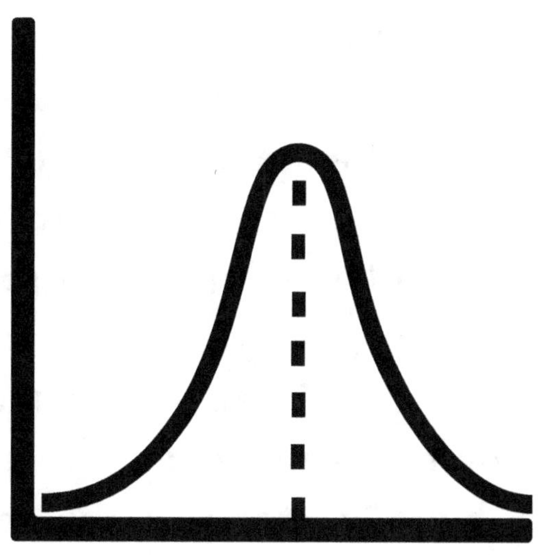

Want some free money ?

It comes with its risks - negligible risk

There are times when you see a volatile week ahead, where there is an event and you cannot predict the direction of the market. You might refrain from trading altogether, or get in a trade that you might regret. You get in, just because you need to be in a trade. It is not recommended, but some people are just compulsive. They need to have a stake in the market. While some are compulsive, everyone goes through that phase some time or the other. Now, when you are drawn to take a trade, you have the choice of taking a low reward high risk trade, that is where people usually end with, or a high reward high risk trade, that is where risk usually eats you up, or a low risk low reward trade. A low risk low reward trade will fetch you very little, but it won't take away anything from you. This will probably block your margins, but return it back to you at the end of the day with a cherry on top. The risk is negligible, but there is always the risk. You look at the spot price of a contract that is expiring today. Then you look at the furthest possible tradable option for the same day expiry, and sell it. Yes, you don't hedge it, but just sell it. Whatever you sell, it will be your gain by the end of the day. Even if you don't close your positions, you earn. Now, while going into this trade, you need to evaluate some factors. You should be at least five percent away from the all time high. You should also be at least five percent away from the current spot price. You can never sell the put option. You need to do this with the call option. For market to fall five percent, it needs one isolated event at a huge scale anywhere in the world, and that is easily achievable, but for the market to rise five percent in a single day, it needs a lot, which frankly almost never happens until there is an event on the same day. Even then, it is unlikely. If something like that is happening, you will have ample time to exit your positions. You will have to keep an eye on the screen, but you can enjoy that free money. Since the contract is expiring worthless, at whatever price you sell that contract, that is your gain. If you want to take more precautions, do this in the last few minutes before closing. You will get a substantially lower price to sell, but there will always be something and the risk becomes virtually zero. It is zero risk, free money, who would not want it, even if it blocks your funds for a few minutes.

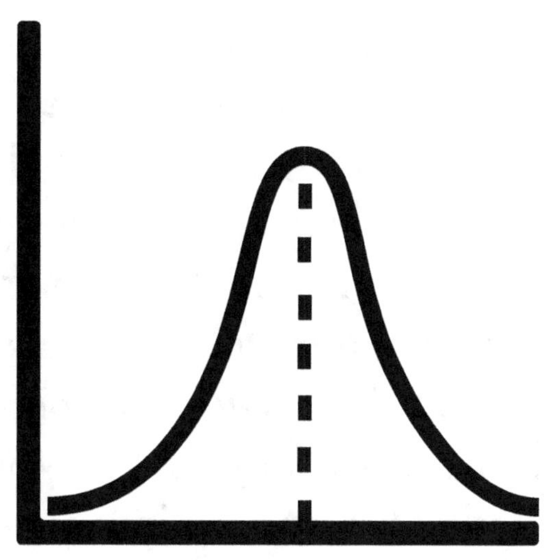

Want to take expiry
date premium

That is a big no

Want to take all that expiry premium home ? Yes, looking at a premium declining ninety nine percent and wishing you had sold that in the morning seems like a really good idea in the afternoon, but that momentary spike that hits your stop loss takes you down. Here, the reward is high, but the risk is even higher. If you are bullish and sell a put option, you need to be sure for the market to stay that way in the next few hours. But, can you predict an uncertainty for the next few hours that even might have just a momentary impact but could last the next few hours. Maybe just a technical glitch somewhere in the world, how do you fight it ? Everything will be fixed in the world by the end of the day, and the impact is just for a little bit and the market will recover in a day or two, but you lose your money and blame it on the event. It could even be some simple profit booking that gets you there. The strike price just above you would show a ninety nine percent decline, while yours would show a percentage of gain that would be your loss, and it could be unlimited. You should avoid zero to date trades, but even if you want to get in, hedge that position with no room for error. Look at the open interest, and hedge it accordingly. A ninety nine percent gain is fun, but a thousand percent loss is unbearable. And, on expiry day, there always is a possibility of a spike. What you are selling, someone is buying. Whoever you are selling the contract to, they are either booking their trade or betting against you. They won't be wrong every time. You don't usually mind being wrong since you have some time to be right, but here, if you are wrong, you are done for. Either sell far Out of the Money options, that are unlikely reachable, but hedge them as well, because they become reachable sometimes or sell deep OTMs on expiry day, which are next to impossible to reach.

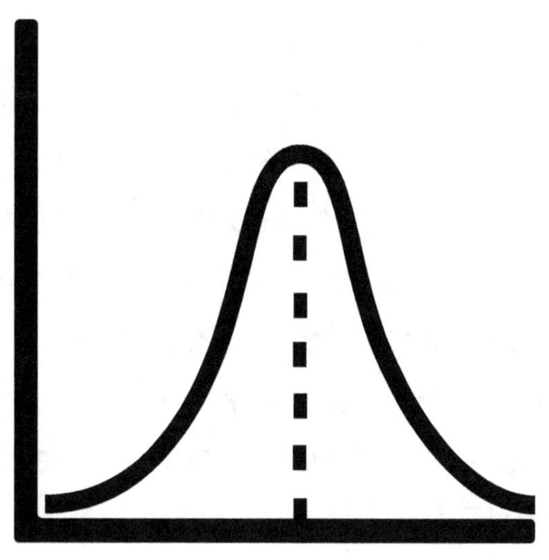

Level up your game

Loss is not an acceptable option

You need to keep trading your small bullish or bearish trades, but you need to level up your positional trades, because that is where the money comes from. This works best after a correction in a bullish market, but can work otherwise too. You see a round number far away which looks achievable in the coming weeks for the market. Now, you think it is achievable, but you are not sure whether the market can take its time to get there. You sell the put option for that strike price months away, and hedge that position with buying a put option for that same expiry equally out of the money. Here, you are selling an In the money option and buying an Out of the money option. Now, it all depends on your evaluation what you earn. If the market reaches your goal in all the time that you have, you earn wonders.

But, even if the market does not reach your target, but starts heading there, you still earn and what you gain keeps increasing as the market keeps heading in that direction and time keeps passing. After a major correction, this does well for selling a put option at the all time high or near the all time high, expecting retracement. You should have time in your corner for this to work and you can exit anytime at your target or near your target. You should always try and keep a few positional trades to do you wonders while you are busy dabbling the at the money trades. Here, you get a lot of intrinsic value as well as a lot of time value. Intrinsic works for you how the market progresses, but time keeps working for you every second that passes. Always keep a trade like this in your strategies while you are wishing for a correction, because a trade where both intrinsic and time value at this scale play together for you is a rare find, and you should not miss that opportunity.

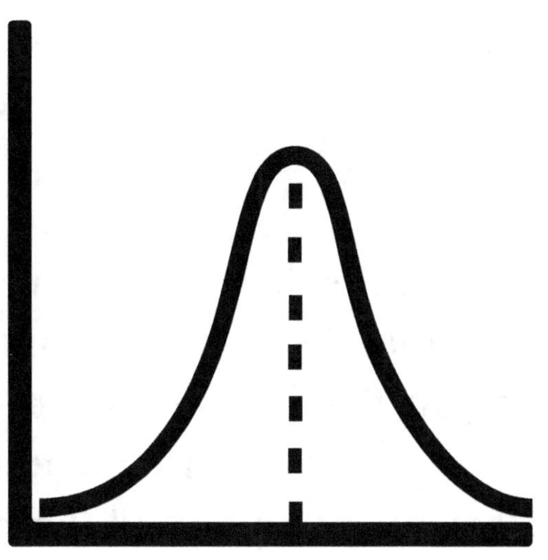

Time

The Three Horsemen

Futures and Options is all about time. The option buyer hates it, the option seller loves it. For an option seller, it is the most integral component. If there was no time value involved, why would anyone sell an option. Every day, every minute, every second, time is working in the favour of the option seller, and you need to control it. If you are selling an option at the current spot price, as long as the market works in your favour, you win, but even if the market does not move at all, you still win. The is your biggest asset when trading futures and options. The premium of theta decay, all your trades should be taken with this in mind. When you are planning a trade, you need to focus majorly on theta decay. Your trades should not be taken on the basis of intrinsic value, but how you can capture the theta decay points. If you are taking a far away trade, you are not working on intrinsic, you are working to capture time. You hedge your position, but you still try to capture the premium, and you are rewarded accordingly. That is why the longer you stay in a trade, the more the gain. Every option seller always imagines selling a naked option, this is a really risky move, but selling it after a major correction gives you a better protection, and a better reward. Think of it as removing the buy component of your trade, and whatever you were spending on buying the hedge, that is also your profit now. For going down this road, never ever sell the put option, because market can crash any day with any event across the globe. If you want to go there, sell a call option, your liability becomes unlimited, but your gain is exponential. If you have your entire margin to risk, this is the best move ever. But, even if the market takes a huge move against you, no matter how momentarily, your positions will be liquidated. So, the choice is yours, this is the best example of a high risk high reward trade, and if you are willing to take the risk, there is no better trade. Here, time becomes powerful, and you own all of it. All you have to worry about is intrinsic value, and even if you are wrong till some extent, time will cover you as much as it can. The only problem comes when things get messy as soon as you get into the trade, this is where you will have a negative position, and there is no end to it. If you have been in the position for a few days, your chances of a loss become highly negligible, but they will always loom.

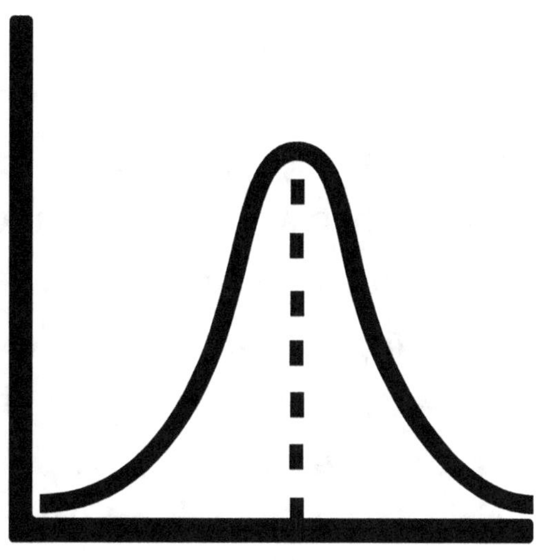

Risk

The Three Horsemen

You are always risking it. If you are taking a trade in futures and options, you obviously understand the risk. No matter how many precautions and hedges you throw in the mix, you know that you are taking a risk. It might be high, it might be low, but there is always a risk, and that is quantified as premium. If you cannot take a risk, you need to play with stocks, where your chances of losing your money are virtually zero, because you can always hold. In futures and options, your contract is going to expire. It might expire tomorrow, it might expire a week from now, or a month from now, but it will always expire and every Out of the Money option will turn zero, and all premium will be gone. That is why you should avoid a buy trade as much as you can, because the system is rigged in favour of the seller. You can obviously hedge your sell, but the risk never goes. And for a non hedged seller, that risk is infinite. There is no end to the liability, but if you are into selling, whatever margin you are paying for your first lot, that can be easily made in three to four good days, and if you are taking a far away trade, you have the room to be wrong, because you will be rewarded accordingly. No matter what, in futures and options, whether you are a buyer or a seller, the risk will always prevail. It will be in the game until a second before the expiry. You can only insure yourself against it. But, this risk can be controlled if you have a directional view of the market. If you sell a farfetched put after a major correction, you are bound to win. When intrinsic value and time value, both start working in your favour, your trading game changes. You take a different prospective on your trading game after that, and it might come with its rewards, but one wrong day can wipe it all out. If you are selling without a hedge, you need to trade with limited lots, with as much margin as you can afford to lose. If you work with that ideology, you can bear the real fruits of futures and options.

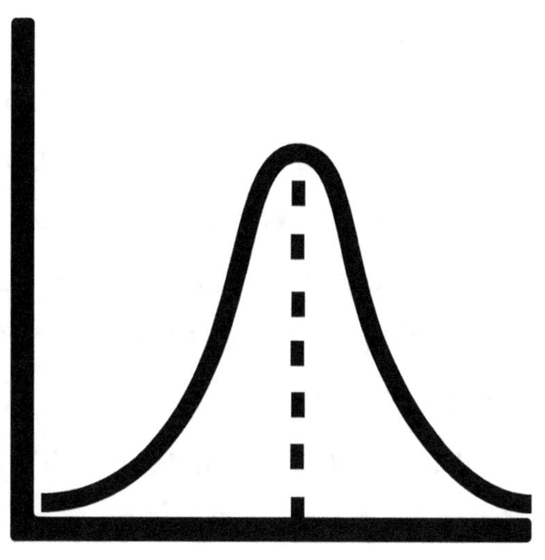

Reward

The Three Horsemen

Reward, every trader is here for that. Everyone goes into a trade, whether it is an option buyer or an option seller to book their profit. The choice while making a trade is what are you going for, a low reward trade or a high reward trade. Low reward trades usually come with lower risks while a high reward trade comes with higher risks. You have to be cautious, because once someone enjoys a successful high reward trade even with the high risks, they become careless, and the market will reward you a few times in your high risk trades, and if not carefully planned, it is going to wipe you off in a single day. Just like selling a put option, put premiums are usually higher and you are attracted more towards it, that is because there is no limit to fall down. Technically, there is a limit to fall down, and that is zero, and there is no limit to the upside. But, the market takes the stairs up, and uses the elevator to come down. Remember that, and stay away from naked put writing. Imagine a war, an attack, a blast, a death, a scam, anything can crash the market in one swift blow. Do you want to be the one who faces that blow ? No matter how farfetched, no matter how secure you think you are, if you are going to sell a put option, you need to hedge while writing it. It reduces your reward, but lets you stay in the game even if the whole world goes against you. Yes, there is risk in writing a call option too, but that risk is predictable to some extent, and you can manage it. Market has a limited bullish trajectory for a single day. It might be a lot, it might dip into your profits, but it will still be limited. The reason behind this is that everyone wants to book their profits at some level, and the sellers are usually waiting for that moment to create an impact. That is why you see corrections from time to time, because the bears get activated as soon as the bulls let it go. Your goal is not to get in a trade, but to get a reward out of every trade you get in.

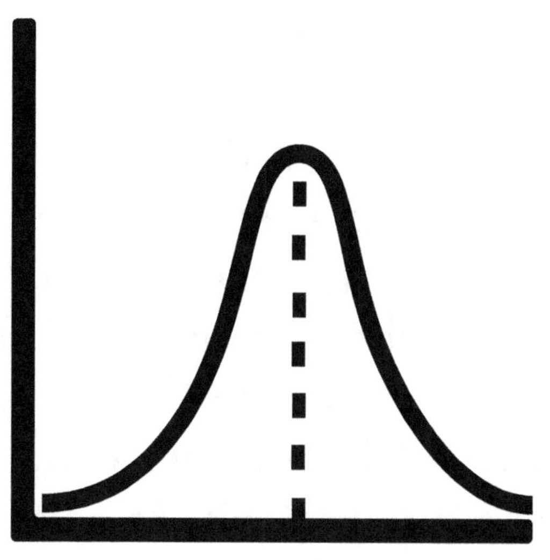

Strategise

For the long run

If you want to be in the game forever, you will have to strategise your trades. You cannot go in unhedged forever. You might win most days, but a single day is all it takes for the game to be over. Pick up the charts and take a look, find those abnormal moves which no one predicted. Most times, it all happened in a single candle with no time for anyone to exit their positions. What if you were there in that trade at that time. If these moves have happened until now, they are going to happen again. That is where the hedge comes into play. It protects you from that single candle move and gives you time to recover. You need to be insured if you intend to play the game forever. If you are here for a single win, sure, play it any way you want. You either win it all or lose it all. But, if you are here to take a dividend, a regular inflow of profit, you will have to go down the hedge route. There will be opportunities where you can sell an option or buy an option and enjoy the ride, but most times, the market is tricky. If it is bullish, everyone anticipates a correction or a profit booking. If it is bearish, everyone anticipates a retracement to the the top. Try understanding that, whatever you are selling, someone is buying and whatever you are buying, someone is selling. If everyone thinks just like you, there should be no sellers or buyers against you, but you are able to trade because someone is betting against you. Don't change what you think will happen, but respect the thinking of the person you are playing with. What if you are wrong and they are right. There is always that possibility. You need to be well versed in most of the possible strategies, because one strategy does not fit it all. At different times, there are different strategies that will fetch different result. If after a correction, you are sure about the retracement, you sell near the top and hedge it accordingly, and the reward will be exponential. On the other hand, if you are still predicting the top, but there is a shred of doubt in your mind as to the when, you take a bullish trade at the current spot price. You need to know what you want from your trade, where the market is, what is the immediate potential, and how you can achieve it with which strategy.

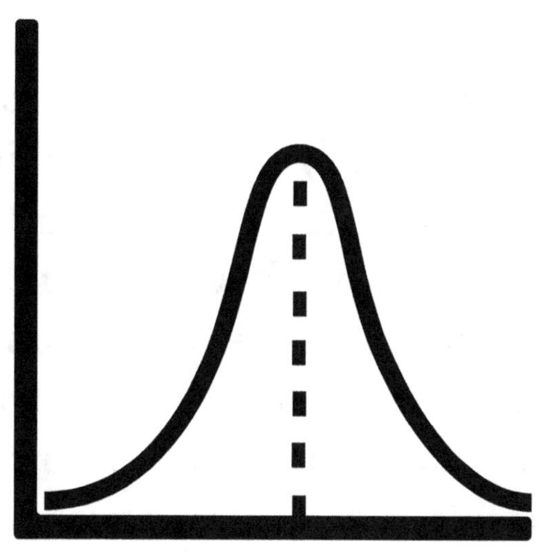

Achievable ITMs

The In the Money diamonds

You are always predicting the market, and in the back of your mind, you know where the market can get to, even if you deny it because it is a direction opposite to your trade, but you always know. You know the most likely bottom and the most likely top. With time in your favour, you can easily capture the high premium on these options. And, you never have to be completely right, you just need that direction and you earn even if the market does not reach there, but moves in that direction. Again, if there is a correction, and your all time high put option becomes deep in the money or the market could be discounted due to an event, and you are almost sure of market regaining its position in the coming weeks. You sell the deep In the money put option, and buy a hedge a little below your spot price. This protects you if you are wrong, but rewards you if you are even slightly right. If the market reaches your target, your gains are exponential, but even near the target, you still earn a good reward. Usually with selling, you earn if the market does not move, but in this case, you either go in naked, or you need the market to move some bit in your direction. You can take a far dated trade, but it still needs to move. Time won't play for you if you are entirely wrong with a hedge. Time will only play if you take a risk i.e. you remove the hedge. If you are confident about your decision, you can forego the hedge. But, if the market has corrected till this end, can you be sure that the market has no more room to fall before it takes a bullish trajectory again. Yes, you will be rewarded even more if the market takes its time to get back, but do you have the holding power in an option without the hedge.

The choice has to be yours, none of them are wrong choices, but it all depends on what is your risk reward appetite. Here, you are not gambling even if you are not hedging because you are certain of the movement, and that too in the long run. But, you have to keep in mind, what if the market falls some more before it is ready to rise. What then ?

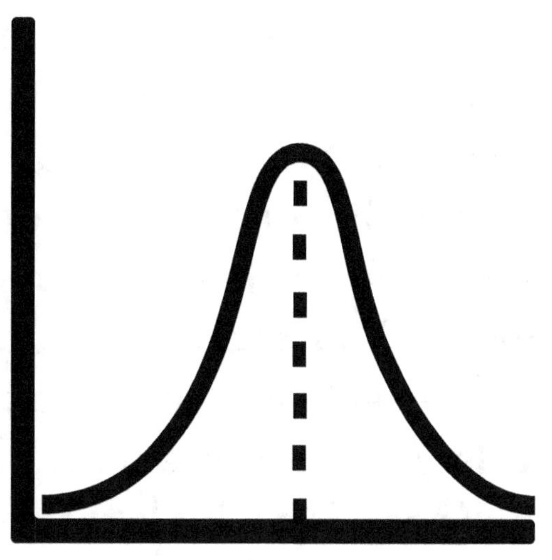

Definite OTMs

The Out of the Money lots

Before taking a trade, you always know the point where the market is not going to reach, especially if you are trading near to the expiry. You avoid these trades because they are not enticing enough i.e. the premium is not high enough. You drop that trade and look for a better one. Now, look at the same trade with a different set of eyes. Your goal here is to look for low risk trades, no matter the reward. These options that you just ignored are Out of the Money, and there is almost no chance of the market getting there until expiry. Here, whatever you are getting is a low risk trade. You might get a lot more a few strike prices above, but that comes with its risks. But, no matter how interesting these OTMs look now, never sell them without a hedge. What you are selling, someone is buying and there is someone, right before expiry, who believes that market might hit that strike price and is betting on it. They are actually paying a premium for buying something that is frankly unachievable, but the market sometimes moves that way. And even if they are wrong ninety percent times, they make so much in that ten percent, that it covers their ninety percent. Do you want to be a victim of that ten percent win rate ? You can sell the OTMs that are near the strike price, but are not achievable, but you need that hedge in place, no matter what happens. On the other hand, if you are selling an option with negligible premium a few percent away, there you can avoid the hedge, and just enjoy the simple low risk premium intake. Even if you check historical data, you won't find a lot of instances with such big moves in a single day without the support of an event. And, even if you sometime get into the wrong end of it, you will see the signs of trouble and will get the time to exit. The market might move up one percent, two percent, even three percent in a short window, but there is always a limit, or a break. You can exit if you sense risk, or ride your free money as you see the other writers burn.

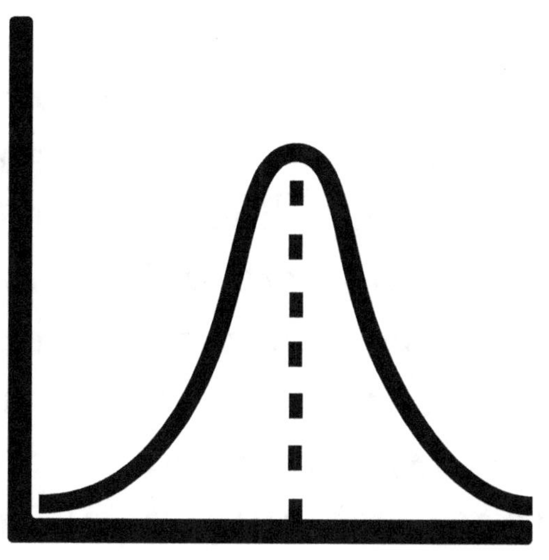

Adjustments

Keep evolving

You might be in a bullish trade or a bearish trade, and you might have ample amount of time till expiry with things working out in your favour, but you never know when they might turn around. If things are going too much in your favour, it is more thank likely that it is time for the market to change course. Now, you need to outsmart the market in this case. If you are in a bullish trade, and the market is highly bullish, you will get a profit right outside of your profitable range if you take a bearish trade. It will cost you nothing, and protect you even if the market starts falling. Think of it as an hedge to your entire trade. Now, you can sit back and enjoy. No matter whether the market is bullish or bearish from here, you are going to win something. This was in case market was working out in your favour, but what are the adjustments needed when the market is not. Here, if you have taken a bullish trade, and the market is taking its time in the opposite direction, take a trade at the current spot price, strategise it so that if the market starts moving in your direction, you start earning more and more. You can enjoy every point until the market reaches your profitable range. Similarly, if the market is out of your profitable range, and you see there is a possibility of it staying there, you put in another range trade whose end overlaps into the start of your original range. This will give you a cover on the downside, a top on the entry of your former range, and a smooth sail from there on. Again, you need to be well versed in these strategies to know which strategy to apply where. You need to back test them before deploying them, you need to know what is the result before you get into a trade. You might know the exact strategy you want to deploy, but the premiums in that strategy at the time you want to enter also play a major role. If you are making an adjustment, you have to try and cover as much ground as possible. You need to profitable in a wider range, even if the profit dips or rises at various levels, but the end result should always be green.

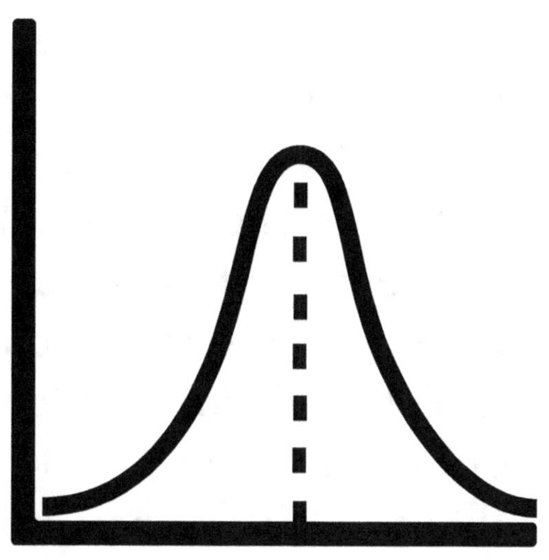

Never overplay your hand

If you want to keep playing

While trading futures and options, it is fairly simple to get carried away. A few good trades is all it takes to think you are invincible. For a buyer, if they got into a trade, and it did not work out in their favour, they increase the lots, averaging out the trade, and with a single point in their direction, they earn more than they would have initially thought. Then they average out more and more, with confidence that the market will turn just a little bit, and they are rewarded accordingly. But the next time going down that course, they have so overbought into that situation, they see big losses with just a little bit downside. Their goal shifts from making a hefty profit to making a tiny profit to making a tiny loss to try and save themselves from losing it all. Same concept goes for an option seller, on a much larger scale, but with a better risk situation. For an option buyer, every second that passes while they are averaging out, they are losing money. But, for an option seller, every second that passes without anything happening, they are earning money. The problem comes in when the movement against you is more than the premium you are supposed to get. Now, even if you try and average out, most of it is intrinsic, that is there to stay, and you are on margin. You might get a margin call, and you are presented with the choice of liquidation or doubling down. Here, you have lost the confidence in your trade, and doubling down does not make sense. Also liquidation in a loss is something that you have never faced before. You decide to skip everything and make a wrong call in order to try and cover your losses, which will put you in deeper. It is not that you will make the wrong call, but there will be so much fear looming over you, that even if the market is making a base to go in your direction, you won't see the signs and believe that you are in wrong yet again. That is how emotions come into play in the market, and that is how people are thrown out of the market. If you have to play it forever, you can never overplay your hand. That gives you the power to stay in your trade, control the situation, make adjustments, bear the loss and even if nothing works out, the strength to come fight again and the energy to live another day. Once you lose it all, how are you going to even enter another trade. Remember it, you need to save yourself the opportunity to screw up again even if you screw up this trade.

Epilogue

The market is not perfect, and it never will be, but trading with a set of rules and strategies can come a long way for every investor. Once you understand the rules, if you have a doubt, read it again until you grasp the core context behind it. But, once you understand them, learn the strategies in 'Strategising the Game of Futures & Options', because there is a different strategy for every situation and you have got to know which strategy works best in which circumstance. Always remember, there is only one primary goal - Never lose money.

Strategies in detail

Strategising the Game of Futures & Options

Stock Market
Rulebook

Playing the Game of the Stock Market

Bill Lucre